A Brixton House production, p
in association with the Mercu

G000154061

# KABUL GOES POP:
# MUSIC TELEVISION
# AFGHANISTAN

## by Waleed Akhtar

*Kabul Goes Pop: Music Television Afghanistan* was first produced by
Brixton House with HighTide, in association with Mercury Theatre
Colchester, and first performed at Brixton House, London,
on 13 May 2022, before touring.

# KABUL GOES POP: MUSIC TELEVISION AFGHANISTAN
by Waleed Akhtar

## CAST

FAROOK      Arian Nik
SAMIA      Shala Nyx

## CREATIVE TEAM

| | |
|---|---|
| Director | Anna Himali Howard |
| Set & Costume Designer | Shankho Chaudhuri |
| Sound Designer | Anna Clock |
| Video Designer | Gino Ricardo Green |
| Lighting Designer | Rajiv Pattani |
| Movement Director | Yami Löfvenberg |
| Assistant Director | Neetu Singh |
| Stage Manager | Sophie Slater |
| Deputy Stage Manager | Ruby Sevink-Johnston |
| Production Manager | Chris Mackie |
| Costume Supervisor | Olivia Ward |
| Casting Associate | Liv Barr |

# BIOGRAPHIES

### ARIAN NIK | FAROOK

Arian Nik is originally from Leeds and studied at Mountview Academy.

Film credits: *Allelujah!* (Pathé); *The Bower* (BFI); *Artemis Fowl* (Disney); *Dating Amber* (Amazon Prime).

Television credits: *The Bay, Van Der Valk* (ITV); *BRUCE, Ackley Bridge* (Channel 4); *Still So Awkward* (CBBC); *Killing Eve* (BBC).

Theatre credits: *The Village* (Stratford East); *The Ugly One* (Park Theatre); *Pufferfish* (The Vaults); *The Last Testament of Lillian Bilocca* (Hull Truck); *Beyond These Walls* (Northern Broadsides).

### SHALA NYX | SAMIA

Shala Nyx is an actor, and creative activist rooted to south east London.

Her most recent work as a creative/actor/writer/activist: *The People's Tribunal: Afghanistan Sessions* co-created with Bezna Theatre and *Sxsterhood: an act of resistance* both for the Camden People's Theatre.

Stage credits include: *A Thousand Splendid Suns* (national tour); *Cookies* (The Theatre Royal Haymarket); *Listen Local* (The Kiln); *The Gravity* (Bristol Old Vic); *Road* (Circomedia); *The Shadow Factory* (The Nuffield Theatre); *Every You and Every Me* (Oxford Playhouse).

Screen credits include: *The Old Guard* (Netflix); *EastEnders* (BBC); *Henry VI* (BBC3); *Bottom Knocker Street* (ITV); *Knock Down Ginger* (BFI Films); *Gifts, I Have Covid* (YouTube Original); *Toxic* (LuxInflux); *Der Grosse Bluff* (Atlantis Film); *Candle to Water* (MUBI) and *Unlike* (Channel 4).

Audio and Motion Capture work includes: *Baldur's Gate III* (Warhammer Franchise); *Octonauts* (Netflix); *Millie and Lou, Corpse Talk* (YouTube); *The Helm of Midnight* (Audible).

Shala trained at The Bristol Old Vic Theatre School.

## WALEED AKHTAR | WRITER

Waleed Akhtar is a writer and actor who was an MGC Futures bursary winner 2021.

Theatre credits include the upcoming *The P Word* (Bush Theatre – Sept/Oct 2022); *Sholay on the Big Screen* (Off Stage Theatre, Bush & Nubian Life); *I Don't Know What To Do* (co-creator – VAULT Festival).

Other work includes: *Famalam* (Season 4 contributor); *Sketchtopia* and *Newsjack* (BBC Radio 4 – Contributor); *Lost Paradise* (short film B3 Media/UK Film Council).

As an actor his credits include *Cruella*, *Salmon Fishing in the Yemen* and *The Great*.


## ANNA HIMALI HOWARD | DIRECTOR

Anna Himali Howard is a director, theatremaker and dramaturg. Her work has been staged at theatres including the Bush Theatre, the Gate Theatre, the Orange Tree and Birmingham REP. She trained on the Birmingham REP Foundry, as the Paines Plough Trainee Director, on the NT Studio Directors' Programme and the Royal Opera House Directors' Course. She was a Creative Associate at the Gate Theatre and is currently an Associate Artist at Brixton House. Her work with international companies includes directing for BE Festival, New Nordics, and the Royal Court International Playwrights Residency. She is interested in new writing, co-creation and working across genres to uproot classic texts.

Anna's work as a Director includes *Curious* by Jasmine Lee-Jones (Soho Theatre); *I Stand For What I Stand On* (upcoming, Strike A Light); *Inside* (Orange Tree Theatre); *I Wanna Be Yours* by Zia Ahmed (Paines Plough/Bush Theatre); *Yours Sincerely* by Will Jackson (Birmingham REP); *A Small Place* by Jamaica Kincaid and Season Butler (Gate Theatre); *Albatross* by Isley Lynn for NEW (RWCMD/ Paines Plough/Gate Theatre).

As a theatremaker work includes *Jane Anger* (Yard Theatre Live Drafts); *Mahabharat/A* by Anna Himali Howard and Zarina Muhammad (Camden People's Theatre); *The Beanfield* by Breach Theatre (New Diorama, national tour 2016).

Anna was Associate Director on *Fleabag* by Phoebe Waller-Bridge (Drywrite/Soho Theatre international tour), Staff Director on *Small Island* (National Theatre) and Assistant Director on *Othello* at Shakespeare's Globe. She is a visiting tutor on MA Dramaturgy at Birkbeck and has been shortlisted for the Arts Foundation Theatre Makers Award 2022. Anna was Senior Reader at the Royal Court and is a reader for theatres and awards including the Royal Court, Bush Theatre, Soho Theatre and the Bruntwood Prize.

## SHANKHO CHAUDHURI | SET & COSTUME DESIGNER

Shankho Chaudhuri is a set and graphic designer based in London.

He graduated from Imperial College London with an MEng in Mechanical Engineering, followed by a joint MA MSc in Global Innovation Design from the Royal College of Art and Imperial.

Previous work as Designer includes: *Traplord* (180 The Strand/Sadler's Wells); *Five Plays* (Young Vic); *Ghost Walk* (Poltergeist Theatre); *Final Farewell* (Tara Theatre); *Inside* (Orange Tree Theatre); *Living Newspaper* (Royal Court Theatre) and *Art Heist* (New Diorama Theatre). As Associate Set and Graphic Designer: *Is God Is* (Royal Court Theatre). As Assistant: *Death of England: Delroy* and *Death of England* (National Theatre).

He is currently Staff Associate Designer for New Diorama Theatre.

## ANNA CLOCK | COMPOSER & SOUND DESIGNER

Theatre work includes: *Electric Rosary* (Manchester Royal Exchange); *The Beauty Queen of Leenane* (Lyric Hammersmith); *Crave* (Chichester Festival Theatre); *Mum* (Theatre Royal Plymouth/Soho Theatre); *Speak Softly, Go Far* (Digital; Abbey Theatre); *Another Planet* (Lakeside Arts, site specific digital); *Mystery Trip* (Nigel & Louise, digital); *Inside* (Orange Tree Theatre); *The Effect* (English Theatre Frankfurt); *Earthquakes in London* (Guildhall School of Music & Drama); *I Wanna Be Yours* (Paines Plough/Tamasha, UK tour & Bush Theatre); *Not F\*\*kin' Sorry, Shuck 'n' Jive, Soft Animals, Fabric* (Soho Theatre); *Groove, Looking Forward* (BAC); *Admin* (VAULT Festival, Live Collision; Dublin Fringe Festival); *Armadillo* (The Yard); *Fatty Fat Fat* (Canada Water Theatre/Roundhouse/Edinburgh Festival & tour); *Mary and Maria* (Camden People's Theatre); *The Butterfly Lion* (Barn Theatre); *Miss Fortunate, Work Bitch* (VAULT Festival); *Twelfth Night* (Southwark Playhouse); *Finding Fassbender* (Edinburgh & VAULT Festival); *Punk Rock, Pomona* (Mountview/New Diorama); *Songlines* (HighTide, Edinburgh & Aldeburgh Festivals, UK tour); *Spun* (Arcola Theatre); *They Sailed Away* (Southwark Playhouse); *This Is A Blizzard* (Waltham Forest Festival/Barbican Lab); *Uncensored* (Theatre Royal Haymarket); *[Blank]* (Orange Tree/Lyric Hammersmith).

As a composer and instrumentalist they have written for the RTÉ Contempo quartet, Tonnta, New Dublin Voices, Kirkos Ensemble, Node Ensemble, Dulciana, Gamelan Nua and their own groups Low Tide and Téada Orchestra.

Trained at Trinity College Dublin, Royal Irish Academy of Music and Central School of Speech and Drama.

## GINO RICARDO GREEN | VIDEO & PROJECTION DESIGNER

Gino Ricardo Green is a director and video/projection designer. He is co-founder of Black Apron Entertainment.

Credits as Video/Projection Designer include: *Edge* (NYT); *Lava* (Bush Theatre); *Children's Children* (Director of Photography/Editor – English Touring Theatre); *Beyond The Canon* and *Poor Connection* (RADA); *Sweat* (Donmar Warehouse & West End); *Passages: A Windrush Celebration* (Black Apron at the Royal Court); *Hashtag Lightie* (Arcola Theatre); Lightie (Projection Designer – Gate Theatre).

Credits as Associate Video/Projection Designer include: *Get Up Stand Up! The Bob Marley Musical* (West End); *Be More Chill* (The Other Palace); *Small Island* (National Theatre). **gricg.co.uk**

## RAJIV PATTANI | LIGHTING DESIGNER

Rajiv Pattani graduated from LAMDA in 2014 with qualifications in Stage Management and Technical Theatre.

Recent design work includes: *Pilgrims* (Guildhall School of Music & Drama); *Sorry, You're Not a Winner* (Paines Plough tour); *Dawaat* (Tara Theatre); *Straight White Men, Yellowfin* (Southwark Playhouse); *Arrival* – (Millennium Mills: Royal Docks); *Statements After an Arrest Under the Immorality Act* (Orange Tree Theatre); *Winners* (Theatre on the Downs – Wardrobe Ensemble); *Final Farewell* (Tara Theatre); *OUTSIDE* (Orange Tree Theatre); *Richard II* (LAMDA autumn season); *Santi & Nas, Omelette, Heroine, Tiger Mum* (VAULT Festival 2020); *Hunger* (Arcola Studio 2); *Dirty Crusty* (Yard Theatre); *Dismantle This Room* (Jerwood Downstairs – Royal Court Theatre); *Wolfie* (Theatre503) *'10'* (VAULT Festival 2019); *Bullet Hole* (Park Theatre Park90); *Babylon Beyond Borders, Leave Taking, Ramona Tells Jim* (Bush Theatre); *Nassim* (Edinburgh Fringe First Winner 2017); *Roman Candle* (Theatre503, Manchester 53Two, Ivy Studio Greenside – Edinburgh Fringe Festival 2018). **www.rajivpattani.co.uk**

## YAMI LÖFVENBERG | MOVEMENT DIRECTOR

Yami Löfvenberg is a movement director, theatre director and a multidisciplinary artist working in the intersection of movement, theatre and cross-arts. Between making her own work, Yami mentors, educates, and delivers workshops nationally and internationally. She is currently the lecturer on the first-ever Hip-Hop module at Trinity Laban Dance Conservatoire. A British Council and Arts Council England recipient, Howard Davies Emerging Directors Grant Recipient, One Dance UK DAD Trailblazer Fellow, Marion North Recipient, and a Talawa Make Artist. She was on the creative choreographic team for the 2012 Olympics Opening Ceremony and is a member of performance collective Hot Brown Honey. Yami has a collaborative company called Passion & Purpose that focuses on dance management, creative projects, and artist progression.

Movement Director credits include: *Human Nurture* (Theatre Centre/ Sheffield Theatre); *Athena* ( The Yard Theatre); *Notes on Grief* (Manchester International Festival); *Rare Earth Mettle, Living Newspaper* (Royal Court); *Fuck You Pay Me* (Bunker); *Breakin' Convention* (Sadler's Wells); *Talawa TYPT* (Hackney Showrooms); *Boat* (BAC).

Director credits include: *Fierce Flow* (Hippodrome Birmingham); *Kind of Woman* (Camden People's Theatre); *Afroabelhas* (Roundhouse/ British Council/Tempo Festival (Brazil).

Assistant Director/Choreographer credits include: *Hive City Legacy* (Roundhouse, Home, Millennium).

## NEETU SINGH | ASSISTANT DIRECTOR

Neetu Singh is a writer, director and theatremaker from Hackney, East London. She is an alumnus of the Hackney Empire's Artist Development Programme and Theatre Royal Stratford East's Young Technicans' programme. She read English at the University of Oxford and is pursuing a Masters in Creative Writing at the University of Cambridge. She founded Haldi & Co Productions, which is now an Associate Company at Tamasha Theatre Company.

# BRIX TON HOUSE

| | |
|---|---|
| Artistic Director & Joint CEO | Gbolahan Obisesan |
| Executive Director & Joint CEO | Gary Johnson |
| Chief of Staff | Nonny Nkomo |
| Head of Finance | Yaw Manu |
| Head of Development | Darryl de Prez |
| Senior Producer and Dramaturg | Ruth Hawkins |
| Creative Civic Producer | Tobi Kyeremateng |
| Head of Communications and Audience Development | Monique Baptiste-Brown |
| Marketing and Communications Coordinator | Amber Hill |
| Box Office & Ticketing Coordinator | Caroline McNamara |
| Head of Technical, Production & Building Services | Richard Owen |
| Technicians | Lee Silcock, Jamie Elford, Alex Ringo |
| Head of Learning and Participation | Oluwatoyin Odunsi |
| Learning and Participation Producer | Kaira Manders |
| Demonstrate! Project Manager | Nicola Rayworth |
| Customer Service Manager | Lili-Mae Billam |
| Duty Manager | Evie Enakimio |
| Tenant & Space Hire Coordinator | Lina Ruales |

**Brixton House Board Members**
(Chair) David Bryan
Abbi Agana
Oladipo Agboluaje
Jacqui Beckford
Richard Beecham
Michael Bright
Sunil Chotai
Fionnuala Hogan
Christina Liciaga
Robin Priest
Carole Stewart
Susan Timothy

**Brixton House** (formerly known as Ovalhouse) opened to the public in February 2022. Our new building is located in the heart of Brixton's local community, and we welcome artists and audiences to enjoy and create experiences in our new home.

Brixton House's **vision** is to create the world we want to imagine.

Brixton House will be a home for a new generation of makers, artists, writers, producers, technicians and audiences. We want our town, city, and its many diverse communities to be reflected in our shows, events and participation programmes regardless of class, ethnicity, language, ability, sexuality or gender identity.

Our **mission** is to thoughtfully curate spaces in which our community can connect, create and enjoy. Community members and artists at various stages of their journey will join us to create and share honest, challenging and innovative work that propels theatre towards a more inclusive global society. Our theatre will be a caring building that supports its staff, nurtures its community and thrives from the creative energy of the artists, participants and audiences who will call it home.

We are delighted to be co-producing *Kabul Goes Pop: Music Television Afghanistan* in our first season with our partners HighTide and Mercury Theatre.

hello@hightide.org.uk – hightide.org.uk

| | |
|---|---|
| Executive Director | Rowan Rutter |
| Executive Director (Parental Leave) | Lindsey Dear |
| Communications and Development Director | Francesca Clark |
| Producer | Holly White |
| General Manager | Hannah Dunne |
| Literary Associate | Sarah Jane Schostack |

**Associate Artists**
Chinonyerem Odimba, Yaz Zadeh, Chris Sonnex, Nicola Werenowksa, Aisha Zia

**Board**
Tim Clark (Chair), Nancy Durrant, Liz Fosbury, Jon Gilchrist, Kate Harvey, Vinay Patel, Leah Schmidt, Matthew Webb

## ABOUT HIGHTIDE

NEW THEATRE FOR ADVENTUROUS AUDIENCES

HighTide is one of the UK's leading new writing theatre companies. Our mission is to develop new theatre productions and programmes that engage and inspire diverse communities in the East of England. We work in partnership locally and nationally year-round to co-produce and tour our productions and celebrate our home. We are committed to innovation and inclusion to widen engagement and raise the quality of our work. Our vision is of an East of England where everyone has the opportunity to share or encounter their story without prejudice and with joy.

We provide a year around artistic development programme, one tour a year and seasonal participation work. Our artistic development programme is dedicated to nurturing diverse talent, creating space for courageous artists to fully express themselves and develop their practice. We regularly tour high quality productions across the East of England, sharing stories and experiences with our local audiences. Our participation work brings together world-class storytellers with communities in the East of England to help them share their own stories and expand their creative lives.

# MERCURY

**Mercury Theatre** is the artistic powerhouse in the East – a vital, vibrant, welcoming centre of culture for the people of Colchester, Essex and beyond. The award-winning theatre presented in the auditorium and in the studio transforms and enriches lives in the local community. Through Mercury Productions and Mercury Originals the company produces world-class theatre, reinventing familiar stories and conjuring bold, new ones. The Mercury talent development programme seeks out fresh voices and stories that encourage people to see through the eyes of others. The Mercury's participation programmes connect communities and celebrate creative potential by providing people with everyday opportunities to be artistic and innovative.

A producing and receiving house with 530 seats in the theatre and a capacity of 96 in the studio, the newly (2021) refurbished Mercury is accessible throughout and boasts a thriving café-bar, dance studio, rehearsal space, participation space and impressive backstage workshop.

Following the major renovation in 2021, Mercury was awarded a BREEAM 'Very Good' certificate, placing it in the top 25% of public buildings in the UK for environmental standards. In 2021 the Mercury was profiled by Theatre Trust as a model of good practice in the UK.

Mercury is delighted to have partnered with Brixton House and Hightide in the creation of this show.

Established in 1937, Mercury is registered Charity Number 232387 and receives regular investment from:

CHURCH STREET
T A V E R N
Premier Partner

Colchester
Borough Council

Essex County Council

LOTTERY FUNDED

Supported using public funding by
**ARTS COUNCIL
ENGLAND**

Find out more: **www.mercurytheatre.co.uk**

**Executive**

*Executive Director* Steve Mannix
*Executive Producer* Tracey Childs
*Creative Director* Ryan McBryde
*Deputy Executive Director* Deborah Sawyerr

**Production**

*Interim Line Producer* Jenny Moore
*Head of Construction* Philip Attwater
*Deputy Workshop Manager* Harriet Wheatley
*Workshop Assistant* Jim Bonner
*Production Manager* Richard Parr
*Technical Manager* Emily Holmden Kingsman
*Senior Technician (Stage)* Roger Mills Lewis
*Technicians* Wesley Laing, Orion Nichol, Darryl Ward
*Company Stage Manager* Rebecca Samuels
*Deputy Stage Manager* Emilie Leger
*Assistant Stage Managers* Gillian McGrath, Lucy Quinton
*Wardrobe Manager* Corinna Vincent
*Deputy Wardrobe Manager* Chantelle Cox
*Assistant Director (Birkbeck Placement)* Michael Cottrell

**Development**

*Development Director* Abbi Roberts

**Creative Engagement**

*Mercury Creatives Project Manager* Joseph Rawlings
*Mercury Creatives Coordinator* Antony Stuart-Hicks
*Head of Creative Engagement* Laura Norman
*Engagement Producer* Elodie Gilbert
*Talent Development Producer* Dilek Latif
*Schools Producer* Forest Morgan
*Creative Engagement Administrator* Una McKeague
*MYC Youth Assistants* Holly Featherstone, Koralia Salacuri

**Marketing**

*Head of Marketing and Communications* Samuel Biscoe
*Senior Marketing Officer* Rhianna Howard
*Marketing & Data Management Officer* Emily Carter
*Marketing & Development Officer* Nathan Garwood
*Marketing Officer (Maternity Cover)* Molly Richardson
*Ticket Sales Supervisors* Rush Atherton, Chyanne Hooks

**Operations**
*Operations Director* Carol Rayner
*Facilities & Projects Manager* Nik Frampton
*Theatre Administrator* Valentina Borja Herrera
*Theatre Administrator (Maternity Cover)* Lorena Saiano
*Operations Coordinator* Jack Pedersen
*Cleaning Supervisor* Edward Cleary
*Line Chef* Andrew Tulloch
*Bar Supervisors* Ellen Duffy, Rhys Lifton
*Kitchen Assistants* David Attan, Drew Pasmore, Ellianna Stewart

**Finance**
*Finance Director* Hazel Skayman
*Senior Finance Officer* Kristin Green
*Senior Finance Officer* Fiona Lucas
*Finance Officer* Stephanie Jones

**Customer Experience**
*Interim Head of Customer Experience* Emma Vidler
*Customer Experience Supervisors* Annaleise Sansum, Rebecca Sykes
*Duty Customer Experience Supervisors* Stefan Davies-Capper,
Eilish Mullane
*Customer Experience Assistants* Jessica Ashley, Aleksandra Astrauskaite,
James Bacon, Richard Bland, Anita Cadogan, Emanie Cherry, Lauren
Coleby, Summer Crosby, Jess Donn, Rachael Fontenelle, Samuel
Golding, Kieron Gould, Clarissa Hankin, Georgina Hart, Caitlin Hegarty,
Sami Hood, Mitchell Howlett, Irsan Ismail, Megan Juniper, Amy Lawther,
Roisin McDonagh, September Mead-Smith, Sarah Mills, Jonathan
Moran, Veronica Morris, Chantel Morrisson, Olivia Ochaya, Kylise
Palmer, Marjanne van der Parker, Brooke Parratt, Calum Rennie,
Maria Rutherford, Leonard Shannon-Bright, Chloe Smith, Jack Smith

# KABUL GOES POP:
# MUSIC TELEVISION AFGHANISTAN

*Inspired by a true story*

Waleed Akhtar

## Characters

FAROOK, *early twenties Afghan male, good hearted, a little vain and self-absorbed*

SAMIA, *early twenties Afghan female, cool and no nonsense (only covers her hair loosely when on air)*

ASIF, *mid-forties Afghan male, to be played by Samia/Farook and lines split as the production sees fit or as attributed in the script.*

## Note on Text

Words in [square brackets] are unspoken.

Off-air/on-air/song are indicated how the production sees fit.

*This text went to press before the end of rehearsals and so may differ slightly from the play as performed.*

*The stage is dark. The on-air sign comes on.*

*An over-the-top theatrical intro skit to the TV programme.*

SAMIA. Where am I? Am I dead or alive? I can't see anything.

FAROOK. Don't worry, child.

SAMIA. Who's that? Are you an angel?

FAROOK. Yes.

SAMIA. But they all said I'd go straight to hell.

FAROOK. What do they know?

SAMIA. What kind of angel are you?

*A light shines on* FAROOK.

FAROOK. I'm glad you asked, I'm a POP angel.

SAMIA. Oh wow. We're all in pop heaven?

FAROOK. Yes! Yes, you are... and it's called *VOX*! The greatest hits show.

*A light shines on* SAMIA.

SAMIA. And what can we expect of this greatest hits show?

*The bright studio lights come on and we're in full show mode.*

FAROOK. It's going to be an hour and a half of musical bliss... as we give you all the latest from Hollywood to Bollywood, to Persian pop, you name it we got it and we don't stop. And the one thing they all want... me, VJ Farook, with the chat and the charts, and the looks that melt hearts. It's time for *VOX*!!

*Off-air:*

SAMIA. Greatest hits shows are lame... where they just play you crappy clips from the past. No one really wants to watch a glorified rerun.

FAROOK. This is different, it'll be more like making the band. Our story.

SAMIA. Okay I'm down with that. So we need to intro me!

FAROOK. No you come later. We actually need to start at the very beginning. Tell it all.

SAMIA. Your beginning.

FAROOK. Well, the story starts with me.

SAMIA. Convenient. So what do I do?

FAROOK. I don't know, watch?

SAMIA. Typical, some things don't change, hogging all the limelight.

FAROOK. That's not fair. Well, not this time at least.

SAMIA. Get on with it then.

FAROOK. You can introduce it if you like?

SAMIA. Gee thanks!

(*Grandiose*.) Let me take you back to a different time, and to a different place...

FAROOK. Now who's milking it? Just the short version.

SAMIA. FINE! Kabul. Afghanistan. 2004. The Audition.

SAMIA *takes a back seat while* FAROOK *speaks*.

FAROOK. 'Farook Issar, my name should be on the list.'

I know it's not, but I'm making the guy look regardless.

Now for my speciality –

SAMIA/FAROOK (*overly dramatic*). 'I spoke to someone on the phone yesterday, he said that I would be put on the list. Unbelievable.'

This is a lie.

The man on the phone yesterday had expressly told me that there was no room at the audition. But this guy doesn't know

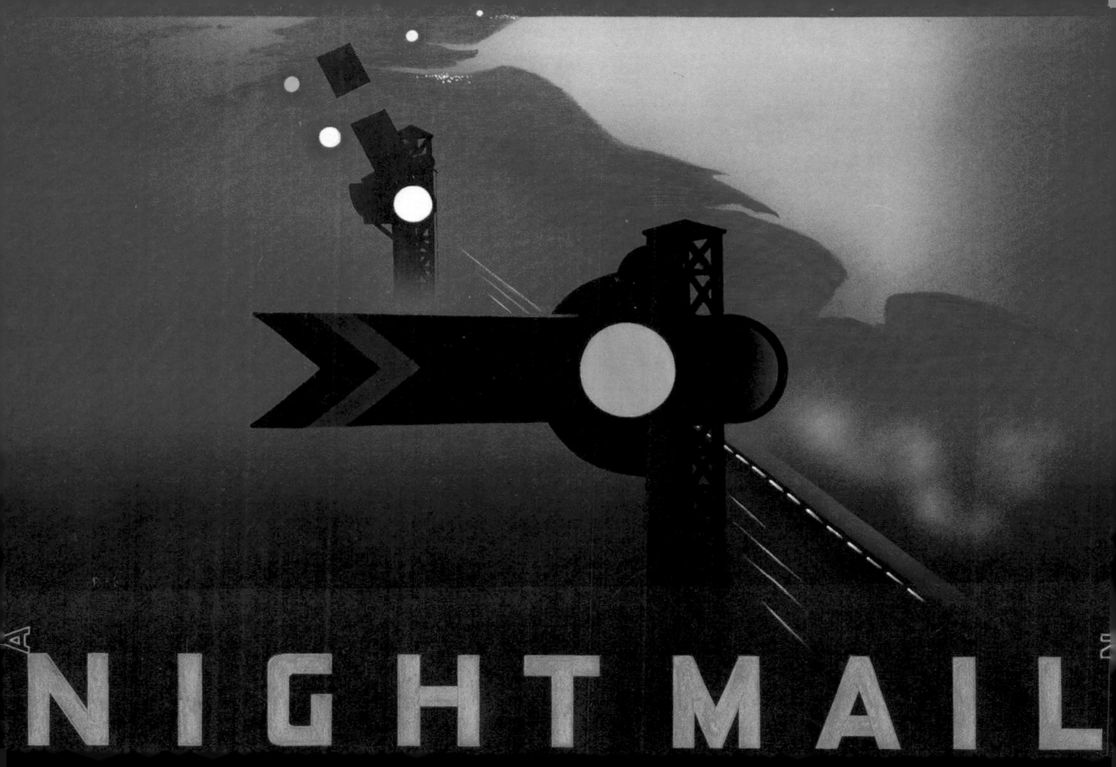
A
NIGHT MAIL

Dear Alison,

Apologies for the delay. Hope you enjoy this — Pip Swallow's suggestion for an AD. We would work with Waleed on the audio reversioning.

All best wishes,

Emma.

www.postalmuseum.org

5 021043 805914

that, and anyway it's Kabul… organisation is no one's strong point.

Now for the charm – (*He smiles.*)

'Can you please squeeze me in?'

It works. It actually works.

SAMIA. I can't believe it.

FAROOK. Neither can I.

Number thirty-three! Step one accomplished. You want something, you go for it, and I want this so bad! To be a presenter on TV. I take a seat and look at the 'competition'.

Number twenty-nine gets up and walks into the studio. He's definitely in his dad's wedding suit from the seventies.

I'm wearing white, all white, white shoes, white shirt, white trousers, white underpants!

*la ilaha illa muhammadur rasulullah, la ilaha illa muhammadur rasulullah*

I am just going to pray over and over in my head to calm myself down.

*la ilaha illa muhammadur rasulullah*

They're all so old, like twenty-eight.

*la ilaha illa muhammadur rasulullah*

It's a sea of bad suits and beards.

I am definitely better looking than all of them.

*la ilaha illa muhammadur rasulullah*

Thirty-one comes out of the studio, it says 'Dolce and Gabner' on his shirt.

Why is he smiling so much? If I had his teeth I wouldn't.

He boasts to Mr Thirty-two, that he's read from an autocue before, so it was really easy.

What the hell is an autocue?

SAMIA. You didn't know what an autocue is?

FAROOK. No.

SAMIA. How much research did you do for this audition?

FAROOK. You either have star quality or you don't… you can't research that.

SAMIA. I spent a whole two weeks prepping mine.

FAROOK. You would. Anyway it doesn't matter. I have a face for TV. Plus I've done radio before, and instead of talking to a microphone it's talking to a camera. What could be easier.

SAMIA. 'Thirty-three.'

FAROOK. My number and I go in. Into the studio…

*la ilaha illa muhammadur rasulullah*

It's not that impressive, basically one giant metal container. Not what I was expecting at all. On the other end of the container there are three of them.

Asif the producer, and owner of this studio, who I spoke to yesterday on the phone.

SAMIA. Our Asif? Man-baby Asif?

FAROOK. Yes, our Asif.

SAMIA. We would call him Man-baby Asif, he looked like a grown-up toddler.

FAROOK. And he would waddle around like one. Giving orders.

SAMIA/ASIF. 'You need to pay attention to what I'm saying.'

FAROOK/ASIF. 'God has given you ears, and big ones, so you should use them.'

SAMIA. No one ever listened to him. And boy would he get frustrated, short-man syndrome. He was even shorter than me.

FAROOK. No he wasn't, you like to think you're taller than you are.

SAMIA. No, people just think that because I have presence, people notice when I walk into a room.

FAROOK. Yeah, they notice but for other reasons... Anyway, we're not doing you yet.

SAMIA. Hurry up –

FAROOK. Asif is dressed, casual? In Western. Beige socks with bata sandals...

SAMIA. Are you going to describe his underwear as well?

FAROOK. Definitely stained.

SAMIA. Okay that was funny. But get a move on!

FAROOK. Basically Asif's outfit is bad... But at least it's Western, so that's progress.

I'm in the room and Asif knows I'm not supposed to be here, in the audition. But doesn't say anything. Thank god.

Two men are sat next to him, I can sense they are the ones I need to impress. Both round, both middle-aged, but well groomed, returned from the West now the Taliban has fallen. The executives of the station.

'Assalamualaikum.'

They nod mechanically.

And then I'm ordered by Asif to speak into the camera.

*la ilaha illa muhammadur rasulullah*

'My name is Farook and I'm twenty-two years of age.'

So far so good.

The bigger of the two men speaks, he's Mr Khalid Hamidi, the owner of the station. He asks me to tell him about myself. So I launch into my favourite subject. ME.

'I've lived in Kabul for most of my life. I work for Rise Radio, and for the last six months I've been presenting a show at night. With music, chat, news, reviews, interviews. Very popular show. Everyone is saying how super-cool it is.

I like Western pop the best, Britney, Backstreet Boys, NSYNC. Everyone says I'm Enrique Iglesias's Afghan twin.'

SAMIA. No one says that.

FAROOK (*ignoring her*). 'I also like to discover new bands, like Westlife, who I think are from the UK? Their song "Flying Without Wings", so beautiful.

*Flaps his arms like Westlife in their video.*

They're the reason I am wearing all white, like the video.'

SAMIA. Why are you flapping like that?

FAROOK. I don't know… It's what they do.

SAMIA. You should stop.

FAROOK *stops flapping.*

FAROOK. Mr Hamidi asks another question about the Americans in Afghanistan.

'I like the Americans, and the best thing about it is we get to eat pizza in Kabul now too.'

Yes! He's laughing. 'And fuck the Taliban.' He's laughing even harder now. I'm on a roll.

I'm back in front of the camera. The autocue. Reading is easy, I can do this.

*la ilaha illa muhammadur rasulullah*

(*Reading badly.*) 'Hello, Salam and welcome all you youngsters. I, insert name, will be your host for the next hour, as I take you… a musical journey. We have a fancy… fantastic programme for you today, and we want you to call in to the show to hear your thoughts about school. What's your favourite subject? I always hated maths. Brackets – Laugh.'

SAMIA. That wasn't so bad.

FAROOK. Don't lie.

'I will do it again, please, but this is not how you talk to young people. This show is meant for teenagers, no? This is like my old auntie talking to me, asking me how school is? Then pinching my cheeks. I can do much better, one more time.'

I did what I had been practising in the mirror all day.

SAMIA. Five, four, three, two, one.

*Morphs into –*

*On-air:*

FAROOK. HEY KABUL!! Who's this guy you ask, with the NSYNC hair and Iglesias's looks? Well, get to know the number one, never number two – VJ Farook. The V is for video the J is for jockey… because I will be playing the wicked tunes, man! Non-stop… So, it's time for Kabul to go POP and the first ever episode of *VOX*!

*Off-air:*

Of course I got the job! Was that ever in doubt?

SAMIA. Yeah, obviously, otherwise the story would be shit.

FAROOK. Monday October 11th 2004, 4 p.m. I go live for the first time to the whole of Kabul…

SAMIA. And for those with good enough TV signal, the rest of Afghanistan –

FAROOK. And one day the world.

*On-air:*

Hold on… Hold on, before we start today I want to be serious for a moment. Please stop the music. Please.

*Music cuts.*

Today in Afghanistan there are many important issues that we are facing in our country, and I want us to look at some of these issues. So I am asking you, the audience, to help answer a very important question. Britney or Shakira? Who is the real queen of pop?

That's right.

So I need you at home to call the studio on six-seven-three-two-three-two-three-two to let me know if you want it – 'one more time', or just 'whenever wherever'.

Farook, you are talking too much? Farook, when will you play some music? Farook, when will you call me? Never.

Okay. Okay. I'll stop talking. And just so you know *who* you should be voting for... Here is one of my favourite songs ever: '...Baby One More Time' by Britney Spears.

*Song.*

*Off-air:*

SAMIA. This was the first ever song on the first ever show?

FAROOK. Yes.

SAMIA. Iconic.

SAMIA *and* FAROOK. LOVE THIS SONG!

SAMIA. The video is amazing too. It's her best.

FAROOK. She has many bests, I like 'I'm a Slave 4 U'. When she danced with the snake at VMAs.

SAMIA. No, this one is the original, and the best. Always, the way she moves, the outfits. You just have to remember the first time you watched it.

FAROOK. That's true. I prayed every night for a month that I could go to an American high school, like the one in the video.

SAMIA. I used to pray that I could just go back to a school, full stop.

FAROOK. Fucking Taliban, under the Mujahideen things got conservative, only religious songs. But the Taliban had to go one further, banning music and TV. We had a TV buried in the garden. But if we got caught... Ya Allah.

SAMIA. What do you know about the Taliban? You and your family ran off to Pakistan.

FAROOK. That was only for a few years.

SAMIA. Some of us stayed here the whole time.

FAROOK. You were always braver.

> *Beat.*

> But we're not talking about that now. We're talking about Britney. Okay.

> I had a VHS of her on the American show *TRL*. It belonged to Imran. I had to promise to do his homework for a week so he'd let me keep it. I still wish I had that VHS.

SAMIA. I had the cassette tape, the whole album. I had to buy it on the black market. I say 'I', I mean my brother. I would listen to this song all the time, lose myself in her voice. I understood her loneliness, her need for something more.

FAROOK. Makes me dream of somewhere else, like the USA, somewhere we could be free. *Vox* – our chance to make that here.

SAMIA. To show a world outside this world.

FAROOK *and* SAMIA. The United States of Afghanistan.

FAROOK. It would be really cool if I could do a Britney backflip into the next bit. But I can't so…

> *On-air:*

> Hey, Voxers, that's all we have time for today, but we'll be back tomorrow, same time, same place, so make sure you are too!! This is VJ Farook signing off.

> *Off-air:*

> Episode one done! And with that a star is born!!

SAMIA. I know what you're thinking, this is Farook exaggerating… but for once he's not.

FAROOK. By the end of the first week I was the superstar sensation of Kabul. It happened so fast.

SAMIA. Afghanistan had never had its own show like this. Like *Vox*. For young people.

FAROOK. So when I went on the street I wasn't ready for people shouting my name. 'Farook, Farook!' 'Hey I love the show', 'You're so great', 'You're so funny'.

I come out of a shop, not even gel in my hair. This little boy runs across the intersection, nearly getting hit by a car, while his mother is shouting at him from across the street. He says 'You're Farook from the TV? Wow. Please can I have your autograph?'

The only paper he has is his maths book. He rips out ten pages, for him and his friends. While his mother is asking him what the hell he is doing.

SAMIA. Don't forget your picture in Dom-min-noors Pizza in central Kabul.

FAROOK. There is a hush when I enter with my friends. I see all the cool kids, but now I'm the coolest kid of all. The owner, he calls me over by name and demands that I have my picture taken with him. Now my face is forever on the wall and I get free pizza every time!

I am not going to lie, I love it.

SAMIA. Who wouldn't? When you are a celebrity, everyone loves you and wants to know you.

FAROOK. Oh and the screamers. Let's do it...

SAMIA. I'm not doing that.

FAROOK. You have to... Please?

SAMIA. Really? Fine!

*On-air:*

SAMIA *is now* CALLER ONE, *reluctantly, screaming unenthusiastically.*

*Off-air:*

FAROOK. Properly!

*On-air:*

CALLER ONE *screaming super-excited.*

Hello, hello, caller number one.

CALLER ONE. Hi... Arghhhh!

FAROOK. Stop now, what is your name?

CALLER ONE. My name is... Arghhhh!

FAROOK. Caller number one, you need to stop screaming
please. I know it's exciting to talk to VJ Farook. But what is
your name?

CALLER ONE. Sorry, sorry... My name is Nazia and I'm your
biggest fan. I like your hair. You have the best hair... like
Nick from Backstreet Boys.

FAROOK. I was thinking more like JC from NSYNC.

CALLER ONE. I am always watching *Vox* because of you.
You're so funny and always smiling.

FAROOK. Thanks, Nazia. And, Nazia, tell me what song you
want to listen to.

CALLER ONE. I chose this song for you, Farook... Just for
you – Farook, will you marry me?

FAROOK. Nazia, you are too sweet. No?

CALLER ONE. Please, Farook, I love you.

FAROOK. Nazia, I love all my fans too. And how can I marry
them all? Even the mullahs are only allowing four wives.
Okay, Nazia, what I can do, just for you... Is play this song
'Shape of My Heart' by the Backstreet Boys especially
for you.'

*Off-air:*

(*Gets out phone.*) Another marriage proposal.

'Please, Farook, please will you marry me, I love you too much. Fatima Xxx'

My third of the day.

SAMIA. How dumb are these girls?

FAROOK. How do these girls get my number in the first place? There is a level of determination.

SAMIA. Don't you mean desperation.

FAROOK. But not everyone loves me, some of the parents are not happy.

SAMIA. It's a parent's job not to like what their children do, right? Everything is too modern, too Western and this is not Afghanistan's culture.

FAROOK. My own parents, they call me and tell me to be careful. I don't listen. My mum says she watches every day and says that all the aunties are asking for my hand for their daughters. I say if they look like Britney then I may consider. Did I mention that the girls love me too much?

SAMIA. Enough already. We get it.

FAROOK. No, I like it here, let me stay here a bit longer.

SAMIA. You're the one who says we have to tell it. So it's time.

FAROOK. For what?

SAMIA. ME! This is where the story really gets going.

*On-air:*

It's the one, the only, the one you crave but will keep you lonely. Kabul's most notorious VJ Samia. The girl they love to hate, but can't nobody hold me down. Here to electrify you with music that will tantalise you. I'll be in your dreams at night to traumatise you.

*Off-air:*

FAROOK. Traumatise you? Like a witch or a jinn? You do that in the daytime anyway.

SAMIA. Not funny.

FAROOK. You skipped a bit.

SAMIA. I was doing you a favour glossing over that.

FAROOK. We have to tell it all.

SAMIA. I mean you don't necessarily come off well.

FAROOK. I deserve it.

SAMIA. I don't know what's worse, everyday Farook or
humble Farook. Okay cool. We're in the office. The
cupboard that Asif insisted was his office. On the TV, the set
looks great, but the studio he owns is shabby. Yet he acts like
it's five stars. TOLO TV, the station the programme is on,
pays him to rent the studio and make the programme, but he
refuses to spend any money on the premises. Or himself.

FAROOK. Cheapskate.

SAMIA. I don't care, I've finally made it into the building.
Months of doing backroom filing and making endless tea to
get to this point.

I got myself a receptionist job at TOLO TV, but I knew the
day I joined that I wanted to be part of *Vox*, I just had to get
my foot in the door. One of the creepy older suits who
always smiles and says –

FAROOK/SUIT. 'Hello, princess.'

SAMIA. – has decided to come with conversation today. I'm
doing my best to be polite, but not really engage.

FAROOK/SUIT. 'They're looking for a woman presenter for –
what's that show for the young people?'

SAMIA. *'VOX?'*

FAROOK/SUIT. 'Yes, yes, I know the producer, I could
introduce. You're so pretty, I'm sure you'll get the job.'

SAMIA. I desperately want to vomit but at the same time ask
him all the details. I know better than to indulge in too much

conversation. So I do a demure look to the floor and tell him 'Thanks, but this is not for me.'

FAROOK/SUIT. 'You're a good girl I can tell, not the sort to parade herself on TV.'

SAMIA. And then he leaves me alone. As soon as his back is turned I'm on the phone to my friend Layla, whose dad got me this job, to find out all the details.

The audition was the week after. I walk in, there are only a handful of women, all 'bad girls' just like me and – as it turned out I was the baddest of them all. I got the job.

FAROOK. So you'd read an autocue before?

SAMIA. Yes. I found out what I needed to know… ahead of time.

FAROOK. Well, it looks like I'm always the last to know everything.

We've been on air for four months and I walk into Asif's office thinking this is another one of his boring meetings, he's not the boss but he has to be humoured. The last one was about how I wasn't allowed to roll the sleeves of my T-shirt to show the tops of my arms. I can't help it if it drives the girls wild. But there she was, all in black.

SAMIA. And there he was like the TV but with more make-up.

FAROOK. It's for the camera.

SAMIA. You keep telling yourself that.

FAROOK. Evanescence knock-off!

SAMIA. What?

FAROOK. All in black, black headscarf, big black DMs, and the eyeliner like a cat. You always know a girl is crazy if she has the cat-liner.

SAMIA. It's to ward off idiots like you.

FAROOK. What about me? First impression.

SAMIA. We've done this game before.

FAROOK. Tell me.

SAMIA. I knew you from the TV.

FAROOK. But first impression in the flesh. No joking.

SAMIA. I've told you before.

FAROOK. Have you?

SAMIA. Too late now, if you can't remember, then I guess you'll never know.

FAROOK. You look beautiful.

SAMIA. What? Are you feeling okay?

FAROOK. Joking aside. I felt it then, but I know it now.

SAMIA. Hindsight... because that was not how this first meeting went down. You look confused by my presence. I can tell by the way you're looking at me, like Bambi with indigestion. Always, your face...

SAMIA *and* FAROOK. I can read it like a book.

FAROOK. 'What's going on?'

SAMIA. And Asif starts. Shall I?

FAROOK. Yes.

   SAMIA *jumps into play* ASIF.

SAMIA/ASIF. 'The show is doing really well, you should be proud, we should be proud, the station is very proud.'

FAROOK. 'Asif, brother, I beg you get to the point.' The man-baby could waffle.

SAMIA/ASIF. 'As I was saying the show is a hit, and we are all proud, but we can't just rest on that. Decisions have been made, we need to keep engaging with the audience, new demographics, expanding our reach. That's why I would like you to meet the new presenter, who will be joining you.'

FAROOK. 'What?'

SAMIA. 'Hi I'm Samia.'

FAROOK. 'No. If the show is doing well then we should not change anything. I'm sorry it's a no.'

SAMIA. 'I don't think anyone is actually asking you...'

FAROOK. 'I am the star, the face of the show. No one else is needed. Okay. There is no point to this meeting.'

SAMIA. 'I've already been employed.'

FAROOK. 'Sorry, if you don't mind we're talking... The show doesn't need anybody, we already have me. And she's a woman?'

SAMIA. 'So there it is. Here you are the new face of Kabul and yet still speaking like the stupid old men. Why shouldn't there be a woman on the TV?'

FAROOK. 'I don't care if you're a woman or not, I'm very progressive. My mother is a woman. I'm thinking about the audience.'

SAMIA. 'Thank you for your concern, but you can keep it.'

FAROOK. 'The show is already a huge leap forward, how are the audience going to react to a woman? They'll think this is too much.'

SAMIA. 'What about the women whose music you play?'

FAROOK. 'That's not the same.'

SAMIA. 'Because they're not Afghan, so you don't own them?'

FAROOK. 'Forget that, I just don't need an assistant to help me.'

SAMIA. 'Well, lucky you have a co-host, and from what I've seen the show could use more of a dynamic, and that's what I'm here for.'

FAROOK. 'The show is doing fine thanks.'

SAMIA. 'What if you're ill?'

FAROOK. 'I'm not planning on illness.'

SAMIA. 'What if you die?'

FAROOK. 'I'm not planning on death.'

SAMIA/ASIF. 'Okay, okay stop! The decision has been taken. I wasn't happy about a woman too. I told them what will people think? A young unmarried woman on TV? But this has come from the top top, the powers that be think it's important, now I have two liabilities. Just both do as I say.'

FAROOK. 'I'm the star, I should have been consulted… Why are you laughing?'

SAMIA. 'There has already been a diva presenting the show the whole time.'

FAROOK. I officially hate her!

*On-air:*

Did you know a cockroach breaks wind every fifteen minutes, that's nearly as much as my Auntie Kadijah… But on today's show we want you to call in with your most random facts! You know the number, six-seven-three-two-three-two-three-two.

AND, we have a special surprise for you.

Welcome, everyone: Samia Razaq to the show, the new assistant presenter.

SAMIA. Co-host.

FAROOK. Yes, yes, like I was saying. My new assistant, I mean co-host, VJ Samia.

SAMIA. That's right, Voxers, it's VJ Samia or you can call me Sammy if you're cute. Talking of cute. I want to play you the new song by Tarkan… Asif the producer said we shouldn't play it because it's about kissing. *Toba Toba – (Expression of repenting.*) But I'm like who doesn't like a kiss, eh? And as far as I care, Asif can kiss my… So here is Tarkan. With 'Kiss Kiss'…

*Off-air:*

FAROOK. Okay, so I might be a little impressed.

SAMIA. Your jaw is literally on the floor… but I have that effect on people.

FAROOK. I mean I can see Asif in the corner of the studio. He looks like a baby about to shit itself. It took me at least two months to build the courage to even remotely defy Asif. It took you like two minutes.

SAMIA. I don't have time, we don't have time, we're changing the world, remember?!

*Song.*

'Kiss Kiss.' This song is a controversial one, 'cause it has the words 'kiss kiss' in it, people see much worse in the Bollywood films they are watching at home.

FAROOK. Everyone loves this song, but it is talking about kissing and some people think that that is against Islam, and you shouldn't listen to such things.

SAMIA. We've moved away from that. So I say they should reread the Quran and spend time worrying about more important things.

FAROOK. It is actually a Turkish song, with the ban on music, musicans fled the country en masse, so there was no Afghan music scene.

SAMIA. Without our own music we borrowed from the best of the rest of the world. Perisan, Bollywood, Western pop.

FAROOK. Western pop is the best. But this song is good.

SAMIA. YES!

FAROOK. Rafiq's is where I would get my cassettes.

SAMIA. The barber's shop?

FAROOK. You could get anything from there

SAMIA. I remember for my birthday my older brother let me have his old Walkman, I spent all my birthday money on black-market tapes. I could listen to all the music I liked, as loud as I liked.

FAROOK. My mum kept saying I would end up deaf. Did you see the video?

SAMIA. Tarkan walking down the street with all these girls running after him.

FAROOK. I always wanted to be him. I mean that's literally me now, with the girls.

SAMIA. Yeah yeah you might have mentioned that a few times.

Back to the show –

*On-air:*

FAROOK. Well, isn't VJ Samia just full of surprises… playing a song she wasn't supposed to. You must give me some warning next time.

SAMIA. Well, it wouldn't be a surprise if I warned you.

FAROOK. Exactly, now you get it.

On with the show… We've been asking you, the Voxers at home, for your random facts. Hey, VJ Samia, here's a surprise. Random fact. Now.

SAMIA. Off the top my head?

FAROOK. Too slow. No problem. Let's hear some of the ones… [you've sent in.]

SAMIA. Stars in space, there are more of them than grains of sand in the world.

FAROOK. What?

SAMIA. There are more stars in space then there are grains of sand in the world.

FAROOK. That's like a school fact.

SAMIA. Still random and still a fact… Your turn.

FAROOK. I said one earlier.

SAMIA. Off the top of your head. QUICK!

FAROOK. Well…

SAMIA. Gotta be quicker than that, mister. If you want to keep up.

FAROOK. NO… Okay… I have one.

SAMIA. Go on then.

FAROOK. Banana… Name of the snake Britney danced with is called Banana.

SAMIA. I mean that's definitely random.

FAROOK. Britney facts are the best facts!

SAMIA. Okay… And now I think it is time to hear what the Voxers at home have sent in?

FAROOK. Yes.

This one is from Khader: the electric chair was invented by a dentist.

SAMIA. As if I needed more reason to hate them.

FAROOK. From Benesh we have: cats can be allergic to people.

SAMIA. I think I am too.

FAROOK. People or cats?

SAMIA. People. I'll read the next one.

FAROOK. Sure.

SAMIA. It's impossible to hum while holding your nose. That's from Omar.

FAROOK. Whaaaat? No way, that can't be true.

SAMIA. Well, only one way to find out. Let's try it. Come on?

FAROOK. Okay, wait, what song shall we hum to?

SAMIA. '…Baby One More Time' by Britney, of course.

FAROOK. On the count of three... one, two, three –

*Both put hands on their noses and try humming... nothing.*
*They look at each other and burst out laughing.*

*Off-air:*

SAMIA. By the time the show is done Asif is still not happy.

FAROOK. When is he ever?

SAMIA. You kind of help me out.

FAROOK. Just call me your knight in Von Dutch armour.

SAMIA. I wasn't expecting it.

FAROOK. I mean even at this point if it's a choice between you or Asif...

I tell him, 'Just stop, you're always moaning. I was going to play the Tarkan video anyway, she just beat me to it. There's no law saying we can't.'

SAMIA/ASIF. 'Laws? What do you kids know of the laws of this land? This isn't America. You should remember what is decent, for all our sakes!' and he storms off, but at least I avoid a telling-off, for now.

FAROOK. I mean as much as I dislike to, I have to admit, you have that something.

SAMIA. What?

FAROOK. That something, star quality, X factor, whatever you want to call it.

SAMIA. Hindsight again.

FAROOK. The audience knows it too. You're a hit.

SAMIA. Not with everyone.

FAROOK. The oldies don't count.

SAMIA. I tell you, 'It was nice of you to help me, with Asif.'

FAROOK. 'Don't mention it, you did good.'

SAMIA. It's a couple of days later when you extend your next olive branch.

FAROOK. 'You can come and help pick some tunes for next week's playlist? Only if you want to…'

SAMIA. 'Yes, thanks, that would be good.'

FAROOK. 'So this machine has lots of the songs loaded. I like to choose older songs too, because most people haven't heard them. And it means I get to play more Britney.'

SAMIA. 'I love Britney.'

FAROOK. 'Me too.'

SAMIA. 'She's definitely the best singer ever.'

FAROOK. 'I mean there is also Madonna?'

SAMIA. 'Their song together "Me Against the Music", I was so excited. And then when I listened to it, I was like, is this it?'

FAROOK. 'No no no… you have to hear this remix. Then you will love that song. It has like an Indian beat –

FAROOK *plays 'Me Against the Music (Rishi Rich's Desi Kulcha Remix)' by Britney Spears, ft. Madonna.*

It's cool, no?'

SAMIA. 'East meets West! This is so much better than the original.'

FAROOK. 'The bhangra flavour makes you want to dance like a Punjabi.'

SAMIA. 'This should have been the main version.'

FAROOK. '"Toxic" too… it takes the music from a Bollywood film. My dad kept telling me when I played it on repeat for weeks.

FAROOK *plays 'Toxic' by Britney Spears.*

Can you hear it?'

SAMIA. 'Yeah, now you say it. We definitely have to add this to the playlist for next week.'

FAROOK. 'Cool.'

SAMIA. 'Which film?'

FAROOK. 'It is from some old Hindi one. *Ek Duuje Ke Liye*.'

SAMIA. '"Made for Each Other", a bit like Justin and Britney.
I was so sad they didn't get married.'

FAROOK. 'No way, I don't like Justin.'

SAMIA. 'You just want Britney for yourself, eh?'

FAROOK. 'No. He is the one who broke up NSYNC, wanting
to be solo, he's not even the best singer, that is JC.'

SAMIA. 'Are you sure that's the reason?'

FAROOK. 'Yes! They were my favorite band. I would do
anything to be a member of NSYNC. They have the dance
songs and the ballads, they are so good. "Bye Bye Bye" –

FAROOK *plays 'Bye Bye Bye' by NSYNC*.

This song, so danceable, simple, but catchy, and in the video
how they're like puppets, on the strings. Then at the same
time they can do amazing ballads like "This I Promise You",
such a beautiful song.'

SAMIA. 'I mean I love NSYNC, but Backstreet Boys? Now
they are the best band.'

FAROOK. 'But NSYNC has the moves – almost as good as MJ
– and the style. Actually don't make me choose between the
two, I love both.'

SAMIA. 'Put on "I Want It That Way".

FAROOK *plays 'I Want it That Way' by Backstreet Boys*.

Now this song is perfect:

"You are my fire
The one desire"

Imagine loving someone that much.'

FAROOK. 'This is on the list for next week too.'

SAMIA. 'YES!'

FAROOK. 'But we need some new stuff as well.'

SAMIA. 'Have you heard of this little group Sugababes?'

FAROOK. 'From the UK?'

SAMIA. 'Yes. Their new song "Push the Button".'

FAROOK. 'I don't have it.'

>SAMIA *passes* FAROOK *a CD,* FAROOK *puts it on.*

SAMIA. 'Track three.'

>*'Push the Button' by Sugababes comes on.*

FAROOK. 'This sounds good. With the videos we don't have, we have to put in an email to TOLO TV. And then they source the videos for us, usually from the US, or they have contacts in India, so we can try for British too. But it's harder. I tried for another British group, Girls Aloud, and nothing.'

SAMIA. 'Okay so this one, if we can get the video.'

FAROOK. 'Definitely. Also you have to make me a copy of this song. I like it.'

SAMIA. 'I can burn you a CD on my brother's computer.'

FAROOK. 'Thanks. This is cool, usually I have no one to talk music with.'

SAMIA. 'Me too… Also Pink, track seven.'

FAROOK. 'No, absolutely no Pink!'

SAMIA. 'Pink is the best.'

FAROOK. 'Have you seen her hair, short like a man's.'

SAMIA. 'If I could be a rocker and shave all my hair off, I would. It's all you or anyone wants to focus on, so why not just get rid of it all.'

FAROOK. It wasn't just Pink, it was Evanescence, Avril Lavigne, I had to always overlook your goth tendencies.

SAMIA. And me, your overly dramatic ones.

FAROOK. How dare you!!

SAMIA. It never feels like work.

FAROOK. But we work hard, you especially. Warming up
before shows.

SAMIA. 'She sells seashells on the sea shore.'

FAROOK. Oh and your big folder of ideas for the production
meetings. I just make it up as I go along.

SAMIA. I admired that, that was your strength. Bullshitting.

FAROOK. Haha. Asif is never happy in those meetings,
especially since we began to team up.

SAMIA. Us against him.

FAROOK. His stupid rules.

FAROOK/ASIF. 'You can't just do what you want! We have to
think of all the people who are watching, young and old, not
push too much or there will be pushback.'

SAMIA. 'Whatever, we know what the audience want, older
people don't even watch the show.'

FAROOK/ASIF. 'They're always watching, that's the problem.'

SAMIA. 'You worry too much.'

FAROOK/ASIF. 'Someone has to.'

SAMIA. Anyway he's not the boss.

FAROOK. The station heads are and they need us.

SAMIA. We've had our time of old people telling us what we
can do or can't do.

FAROOK. It's our time to make the rules.

SAMIA. Or break them.

FAROOK. For the love of god I will roll my sleeves up if
I want to. (*Rolls his sleeves.*)

*On-air:*

SAMIA. It's time to play the fart game.

FAROOK. Where we replace one word of the title of a song with the word 'fart' and you get to choose your favourite.

SAMIA. And the track we play next.

FAROOK. Okay, so here goes, in no particular order, here are the runners-up:

SAMIA. 'Shape of my Fart' – by BSB.

FAROOK. 'Baby One More Fart' – from my future wife Britney.

SAMIA. How dare you desecrate Britney!

FAROOK (*sings*). 'My loneliness is killing me (and I) I must confess I still believe (still believe)'

Come on. I know you know the words.

SAMIA. Umm… Sure.

SAMIA, *reluctant, joins in and then gets into it.*

'When I'm not with you I lose my mind Give me a sign Hit me, baby, one more time.'

The best song. 'Don't Fart' – by No Doubt.

FAROOK. 'Uptown Fart' – Westlife.

SAMIA. 'I'm Like a Fart' – Nelly Fartado.

FAROOK. But my winner is – 'My Fart Will Go On' – by Celine Dion.

SAMIA. My favourite is – 'Spice Up Your Fart' – Spice Girls.

SAMIA *clocks* ASIF *in the studio, forcing them to a break.*

But before we announce who you chose as the winner we are going to an ad break.

FAROOK. See you on the other side!

*Off-air:*

SAMIA. Asif has forced us to ad-break and is giving us his look of disgust. We're used to it.

FAROOK. He didn't want us to play this game

SAMIA/ASIF. 'What are you teaching the children?'

FAROOK. So obviously we had to.

SAMIA. Plus we thought it was funny.

FAROOK. But it's not just that.

FAROOK/ASIF. 'You were singing on the TV, you go too far. You are Afghan, not the people in your videos.'

SAMIA. 'Don't you think you we know that.'

FAROOK/ASIF. 'Sometimes I think you forget. Samia, remember you're a woman, they already have a reason to hate you, don't give them any more.'

SAMIA. 'Chill out, I was barely humming along, you don't need to worry.'

FAROOK. 'I made her.'

SAMIA. 'No you didn't, I make my own choices.'

FAROOK. 'It was harmless, and the backwards people don't matter now.'

SAMIA/ASIF. 'And where do you think these "backwards people" have gone? A fish with teeth tastes the same as a fish without.'

FAROOK. We both try not to laugh, what does that even mean?

SAMIA. Is he hungry?

FAROOK. Is he having fish for dinner?

SAMIA. He's a fine one to be coming out with all this morality, he's happy enough to be making money from playing music, us, the show.

FAROOK. Maybe we should have listened more. We were lucky, we slipped things by.

SAMIA. Nothing happened. This is what the people want now. FUN.

FAROOK *and* SAMIA. United States of Afghanistan!

SAMIA. If we'd listened to Asif the show would have been boring.

FAROOK. But.

SAMIA. No buts…

*On-air:*

And we have a winner?

FAROOK. What song will we be playing for you – will it be 'My Fart Will Go On' or –

SAMIA. – or 'Spice Up Your Fart'?

FAROOK. With a staggering eighty-eight per cent of the vote it's Celine Dion…

*Song.*

SAMIA. Not fair. This song was always going to win. Regardless of the fart.

FAROOK. The whole of Afghanistan went crazy for this song and even years later they still love it.

SAMIA. And the movie. Jack and Rose, every girl wants to marry Jack.

FAROOK. And every boy wants to be him.

SAMIA. All the boys trying to have Jack's hair with the fringe coming down the front.

FAROOK. I admit it I did too, at school.

SAMIA. I can't say I'm surprised.

FAROOK. But my mother freaked out and said I would just get in trouble with the Talib so she cut it for me herself. I had to go to school looking like I was wearing a wig.

SAMIA. Sounds like she did you a favour.

FAROOK. You can still buy *Titanic* T-shirt, shoes, make-up, flip-flops, *Titanic* rice –

SAMIA. *Titanic* hijab…

FAROOK. I begged my mum and dad to buy all this stuff.

SAMIA. Also every wedding I went to – *Titanic*-shaped cake. It's not a good omen for a wedding, it's not going to end well.

FAROOK. Why do Afghans love this film so much?

SAMIA. It has everything: the love, the drama like our lives… This is how an Afghan loves forever, and how they hate forever.

FAROOK. Also there was enough space for Jack on that plank, she could have shared.

*Off-air:*

SAMIA. The speed at which my life changes. I'm famous now too. And it's good – no, it's better than good it's AWESOME.

FAROOK. That's because we're not just famous, we're superstars.

SAMIA. We're making money.

FAROOK. I can buy all the things I want, no more clothes from the market. I can go straight to the mall.

SAMIA. I can help pay for my brother's education. He's the smart one. But the people recognising you in the street.

FAROOK. Acting like they know you.

SAMIA. These little girls coming up to me, saying 'I want to be just like you when I grow up'. It makes me so happy. A nation of women who will be seen, who will take inspiration… from me.

FAROOK. I'm from the Hazara caste and some people don't consider us real Afghans, so now because I'm famous, I'm

like, 'Forget you. Your daughter wishes she could marry
a Hazara.'

Know what's better than being a superstar? Having a friend
to share it with.

SAMIA. We're in this together.

FAROOK. There is our interview which makes the front page of
the *Afghan Times*.

SAMIA. With the headline 'The Notorious Two'. And a picture
of me and you standing back to back.

FAROOK. We look super-cool. I still have that picture.

SAMIA. Love us or hate us, but you can't ignore us.

FAROOK. Everything we do makes waves. I wear a bandanna.

SAMIA. You look like a pirate.

FAROOK. But you know what, the next day all the boys in
Kabul look like pirates too.

*On-air:*

Hey Sammy we just played the number two video and it
looks like Kelly Clarkson is still not 'gone' from number two
to number one, with 'Since You've Been Gone'.

SAMIA. Wow that was a bad joke even by your standards.

FAROOK. Poor Kelly. Like the sister no one wanted to marry,
but I say it's better to be 'Miss Independent' anyway. See
what I did there? But 'Don't Cha' want to know who is the
new number one?

SAMIA. Yes, yes, yes!

FAROOK. Well, it's The Pussycat Dolls.

SAMIA. Wow, my new favourite group.

FAROOK. They have the moves.

SAMIA. And the looks, the main one looks Afghan, no?

FAROOK. Pakistani maybe?

SAMIA. I did my hair like her.

SAMIA *pulls her scarf down*.

FAROOK. I can see, and so can everyone at home.

SAMIA. It's 2005, times have changed now.

FAROOK. It looks nice.

SAMIA. It's dead straight, I'm using GHD irons, all the girls are using them now.

FAROOK. Maybe I can borrow?

SAMIA. You want to look like a Pussycat Doll too?

FAROOK. NO!

SAMIA. You'd look very pretty.

FAROOK. I just want to use a little here on my fringe. But we're almost out of time, so let's play this week's number one 'Don't Cha'. See you tomorrow for more music and mischief.

*Off-air:*

'Your hands are shaking.'

SAMIA. 'It's nothing.'

FAROOK. 'Are you okay?'

SAMIA. 'Yeah, yeah, it's just [the reaction]… I'm being silly. I'll be fine.'

FAROOK. 'Sure sure?'

SAMIA. 'Yeah! United States of Afghanistan!'

FAROOK. I shouldn't have let it slide.

SAMIA. But you did, and seriously, I'm fine. And with that I am one of the first women on Afghan TV to show their hair, not to wear a scarf, and wear Western dress. I'm branded a whore or the new face for women in Afghanistan, depending on who you ask.

FAROOK. Asif is surprisingly subdued about it all.

FAROOK/ASIF. 'Just because you can doesn't mean you should. People are not happy, they're calling you a scandal queen.'

SAMIA. 'None of this is for attention.'

FAROOK/ASIF. 'That's not what it looks like to the public.'

SAMIA. 'The TOLO TV execs think it is a great idea.'

FAROOK/ASIF. 'And they know best? Take it from someone who is wiser, go slow.'

SAMIA. And he shakes his head. He knows not to push it, the ratings go up, which means more money in his pocket.

FAROOK. He was right, the hard-line religious clerics hate us.

SAMIA. Ignorant. They hate everyone. But the laws have changed so what can they do?

FAROOK. They have influence, people still listen to them.

SAMIA. Not the young people, the young people love us. And that's who's making the future.

FAROOK. Us. The young people.

SAMIA. We are free to do what we want now, no one is paying attention to the old men. They grumble about everything. But they have lost their power. The new Afghanistan is finally here.

FAROOK. We're invited to the annual TOLO TV party.

SAMIA. I've never been to a party like this. The room is full of the most glamorous people.

FAROOK. And stinks of money. All the men in suits and their wives.

SAMIA. Who look at me a bit funny.

FAROOK. There are internationals here too, people from the US.

SAMIA. We all knew the station was funded by America, so there was definitely money. They'd won the war and now they were trying to win the minds and hearts of the people by using the TV.

FAROOK. By using us?

SAMIA. We both know what we're doing.

FAROOK. Do we?

SAMIA. Yes, America is a force for change. We want to be part of that. Don't try and change it, it's not the place for hindsight.

FAROOK. The 'United States of Afghanistan'.

SAMIA. Yeehaa!

FAROOK. Some people are even drinking at this party. I've never been around alcohol in my life.

SAMIA. Someone offers me a drink.

FAROOK. Don't.

SAMIA. I'll do what I want.

*Beat.*

But, I take a juice instead.

FAROOK. Everyone is watching.

SAMIA. Everyone else at the station is just jealous. The young stars, with the highest rated show.

FAROOK. The head of TOLO TV calls me over personally to have a private chat, he's with an American. He tells me he is proud, we must keep doing what we're doing – can't wait to tell Asif – and that if I needed anything I must call him direct on his cell and hands me his card.

The American says 'Good work, buddy,' and I feel like I'm in a movie.

SAMIA. He doesn't speak to me personally.

FAROOK. Probably because it's not appropriate.

SAMIA. What?

FAROOK. Just that it doesn't look good, for a man to be talking to an unmarried woman privately.

SAMIA. Bullshit.

The show's budget has increased. We give away T-shirts that say 'VOX'!

FAROOK. We do outside broadcasts.

*On-air:*

SAMIA. I'm here in Kabul Zoo. We remember one of the city's most famous residents, Marjan the lion. But first we have a hot interview for you, I'm here in the monkey enclosure to interview Maqbool the monkey on all things pop.

*Off-air:*

Go on.

FAROOK. You can't be serious?

SAMIA. I am.

*On-air:*

So, Maqbool, who is better, Christina or Britney?

FAROOK *makes monkey noise.*

Britney, I see you have taste. Will BSB make it to number one?

FAROOK *makes monkey noise.*

No? We'll find out for sure at the end of the show. Okay, next question –

*Off-air:*

FAROOK. Enough.

SAMIA. Don't forget my favourite.

*On-air:*

FAROOK. I'm on the streets of Kabul. As today we are going to give one lucky guy a makeover in a segment that we are calling: 'From Mullah to Movie Star'.

*Off-air:*

SAMIA. I loved that Mullah to Movie Star, one of your best ideas.

FAROOK. Why thank you. It was always amazing. Shave a beard, a little bit of hair gel, some jeans and a T-shirt. Voilà.

SAMIA. They look so much better at the end.

FAROOK. But the people were the same.

SAMIA. Stop.

FAROOK. We thought we were indestructible.

SAMIA. This… it's new, it wasn't there at the time.

FAROOK. I wish it had been.

SAMIA. You can't change it now. You enjoy it as much as I do. We know the station needs us and we know just how much to push. Asif tries to tame us, but he's all bark and no bite now, so we have as much FUN as possible!

FAROOK. Me and Sammy are cruising around the city.

SAMIA. Woohooo!

FAROOK. Did I mention that I have a car now… yeah, it's a convertible. Imported, Toyota.

SAMIA. Jamie, I loved Jamie Lynn.

FAROOK. We named her after Britney's little sister, Jamie Lynn Spears.

SAMIA. You came to pick me up, you'd just got the car. It's love at first sight. I insist we drive with the top down.

FAROOK. 'It's not warm enough and my hair will get messed up.'

SAMIA. 'I don't care, I want the top down.'

FAROOK. We cruise around for hours, with music bursting from the speakers.

SAMIA. 'Let's Get It Started' by the Black Eyed Peas is on repeat.

FAROOK. I'll never forget the summer of Jamie Lynn. Sometimes I close my eyes and I'm back there: steering wheel in my hand. Music on the stereo and the mountain roads ahead. Just me and you.

SAMIA. I promise myself that I'm going to learn how to drive.

FAROOK. We park somewhere high in the mountains.

SAMIA. A view of the whole city.

FAROOK. Our city.

SAMIA. Kabul.

*Beat.*

FAROOK. It's now nearing the end of the summer.

SAMIA. But it's still super-hot.

FAROOK. We're riding around in Jamie Lynn. The breeze in our hair.

SAMIA. We're in the front and our friends are in the back seat and we're all singing.

FAROOK. You know that old song, the 'Kids in America', me and Sammy would sing it –

SAMIA. But we changed it, the lyrics, to Afghanistan.

'We're the kids in *Afghanistan* – whoa!
We're the kids in *Afghanistan* – whoa!'

FAROOK. We are though, we are the kids of Afghanistan...

SAMIA. We are young and free and I feel it, the possibility to do anything, to be anyone. I love it as much as I love this city.

FAROOK. We stop at a traffic light, and a car pulls up beside us.

SAMIA. We're happy, just leave it there.

FAROOK. They are saying something so I turn the music down.

SAMIA. Stop, you're making a big deal out of nothing. I dealt with this kinda thing before.

FAROOK. There are two bearded men in the car, they're both young and seething with rage. 'You're the devils off the TV.'

I ignore them.

And then they turn to you and yell 'slag' in Pushto, chucking a bottle of Pepsi right at you. Your top is drenched,

SAMIA. I yell after them, 'Your mother is a slag and her mother too.'

FAROOK. We're all silent. The lights turn, you instruct me to drive. You turn up the music and pull off your cardigan, throw it up in the air, allowing it to drift off behind us. Then you sing even louder.

SAMIA. 'We're the kids in Afghanistan – whoa!
We're the kids in Afghanistan – whoa!'

FAROOK. Like nothing ever happened.

*On-air:*

Time to play 'Get to Know'.

SAMIA. We are going to find out who knows the other one better. Me or Farook, with questions from you the audience at home, that we have to answer about each other.

FAROOK. Whoever wins gets to make the other wear the dunce's hat.

SAMIA. Get ready to sit in the corner, fool. Question one, how many brothers and sisters do you each have?

FAROOK. Well, Samia has four brothers.

SAMIA. Correct.

FAROOK. She's the only girl. Explains a lot.

SAMIA. Farook has one older brother. He's the only girl too.

FAROOK. HAHA funny.

SAMIA. Next question –

FAROOK. Who do you each think is the best pop star?

SAMIA. Easy.

SAMIA *and* FAROOK. Britney Jean Spears.

FAROOK. We both said the same.

SAMIA. What is your favourite food? Farook's is pizza.

FAROOK. YES! Yours is… Ashak.

SAMIA. Wrong. Mantu.

FAROOK. Damn. Next question: When did you get your first text?'

SAMIA. What?

FAROOK. I got mine the morning after the car. 'Motherfucker, son of a whore. You're a disgrace to Afghanistan, we will find you and end you.' When did you get your first text?

SAMIA. This is not how the game went.

FAROOK. Forget the game. I failed. I don't know what your favourite colour is, and that means I spend the rest of the show with the dunce's cap on my head. You can't help smiling from ear to ear…

I don't care about the game. When did you get yours, your first text?

I don't know, because I never ask. I never ask you:

When did you get your first text? When did the cursing start on the street? The shouting? Are you ever scared? How did you get so good at hiding it?

SAMIA. And you want me to answer now?

FAROOK. Yes.

SAMIA. You know I can't.

But maybe I'd tell you that for a woman those texts have always been there in one shape or another. None of this is anything new.

FAROOK. We were stupid.

SAMIA. Or brave, sometimes it can be the same thing.

FAROOK. A month later Jamie Lynn is stolen. Did they know it was my car? She's found burnt-out and abandoned on the outskirts of the city.

SAMIA. She faced the most Afghan of deaths for a woman, immolation. Burned alive.

FAROOK *puts the dunce's hat on.*

*On-air:*

FAROOK. To end today's show we have the beautiful ballad 'Hero', by my Latino twin, Enrique Iglesias.

*Song.*

This is a beautiful song. It's one of my favourites.

SAMIA. You don't look like him.

FAROOK. What! We're both brown, and handsome. He's me if I wasn't born here.

SAMIA. I don't like this song.

FAROOK. I know, but you used to.

SAMIA. Then I actually paid attention to the lyrics.

FAROOK. It's about love.

SAMIA. And all the woman does is stand there and take his breath away. What happens when she gets old? He moves on to the younger one to take his breath away.

FAROOK. He will love her forever. He would do anything for her.

SAMIA. Why does she need a hero? I don't want a hero, I want to be my own hero.

FAROOK. You would.

SAMIA. We've been told to play more male singers. Asif gave us a list of songs to avoid. All women.

FAROOK. 'Britney is on the list. No way!'

SAMIA/ASIF. 'Calm down. I know you don't think so but I'm on your side. What I say is for your own good and now you need to compromise, okay.'

FAROOK. 'No Britney, absolutely no way!'

SAMIA/ASIF. 'You want a show? Now is not the time to push, look at the world outside, the West is not in favour and that's what this show is, so we tone down.'

SAMIA. 'To appease the men we silence the women.'

FAROOK/ASIF. 'Not silence, reducing. One woman a show and we have to have shorter videos and more Bollywood.'

SAMIA. 'We're not actually going to do it?'

FAROOK. 'I'm not sure? I mean, okay for a while, as long as we get to keep Britney.'

SAMIA. We have been ordered to remain in the studio building. Second time this week. Wait for the 'all clear' before we can leave.

FAROOK. The one thing Asif doesn't skimp on is security, guards and reinforced concrete surround the compound.

SAMIA. This time it's an actual suicide-bombing in the main shopping area in Kabul, fifty people dead so far.

FAROOK. The Taliban. Why won't they just die?

SAMIA. It's like the end of a horror movie when the hand pops out of the grave to remind you: you are never really safe, never really free.

FAROOK. The Taliban are still very much a force.

SAMIA. Mainly outside of Kabul.

FAROOK. Not just outside. Here, in our Kabul too.

SAMIA. We hoped that with the Americans the bloodshed would stop.

FAROOK. Now it feels like the city is even less safe, you don't know who is working with them, or when they will strike next.

SAMIA. 'I've got to get out of here.'

FAROOK. 'You're not the only one, I've got a hair appointment. I want something a bit more Ricky Martin, I think it's time to move on from JC.'

SAMIA. 'Sometimes you amaze me.'

FAROOK. 'Thanks.'

SAMIA. 'I was being sarcastic.'

FAROOK. 'Yeah I got that, Sammy.'

SAMIA. 'Your family don't live in the city any more. Mine do. I need to know they're okay.'

FAROOK. 'Sorry, sorry, have you called home?'

SAMIA. 'I forgot my cell.'

FAROOK. 'Here, just use mine. Don't worry, they'll all be fine.'

*Pulls out his phone.*

SAMIA. 'What is it?'

FAROOK (*reading*). '*America's cocksucker, traitor, son of a whore.*'

SAMIA. 'That's a funny proposal.'

FAROOK. 'I don't get it.'

SAMIA. 'Just ignore it, I get them all the time.'

FAROOK. 'I changed my number two days ago, no one has it.'

SAMIA. 'Are you scared?'

FAROOK. 'No, but there would be no shame if I was.'

SAMIA. 'Phone.

> FAROOK *hands over his cell.*

> Salam, is everyone okay?... Don't worry, don't worry...
> Have you called the school? His friends?... He'll be okay...
> No. We can't leave... As soon as I can, okay.'

FAROOK. 'What's going on?'

SAMIA. 'He hasn't come home, my little brother, and no one has
heard from him. Sometimes after class they go to the mall.'

FAROOK. 'I'm sure he's okay, he's probably just caught up in
all this trying to get home.'

SAMIA. 'You don't know that. If anything's happened to him.
I couldn't... I don't know what...'

FAROOK. 'Don't think like that.'

SAMIA. 'I can't just sit here and do nothing. I have to go.'

FAROOK. 'You can't. Please, it's not safe.'

SAMIA. 'I don't have a choice... And when it's written it's
written.'

FAROOK. 'But you can't be reckless, we have to be smart.'

> I don't get a chance to say that, she's gone, out of the studio,
> into the world.

SAMIA. Head on.

FAROOK. Always your way. And I'm left feeling slightly
ashamed, waiting for Asif to say it's safe to leave the building.

SAMIA. It was a broken leg and some cracked ribs, caught in
the stampede fleeing the mall, but he's alive. I hug him so
tight I almost crack another rib.

FAROOK. I was right when we first met. We were never equal.

> You were better than me, braver than me. I was a man
> making a stand in a man's world. You were a woman

standing up in that same world. If they hated me they hated you more. I can see that clearly now.

SAMIA. There is that hindsight again.

FAROOK. I've just got to the studio and you are already in Asif's office. 'What's going on?'

SAMIA/ASIF. 'There was a threat made to the TOLO headquarters.'

FAROOK. 'What kind of threat?'

SAMIA/ASIF. 'It was a hoax… A package addressed to our show… It seems that audiences are not responding to elements of the show as well as they used to. So we need to make more changes.'

SAMIA. 'You mean I need to make changes.'

FAROOK/ASIF. 'Maybe you can talk some sense into her.' And Asif leaves.

SAMIA. 'They want me gone. One little threat to them and they can't handle it.'

FAROOK. 'What are you talking about?'

SAMIA. 'Asif told me I need to cover my hair properly and stop wearing Western clothes, or they will have to tell me to leave.'

FAROOK. 'He doesn't have the power…'

SAMIA. 'Like he couldn't with the music?'

FAROOK. 'We're still mainly playing what we want.'

SAMIA. 'This hasn't come from him, he was relaying a memo from the TOLO executives. Why don't I read it for you.

SAMIA *pulls out a memo.*

"*We really appreciated the hard work you have put into* Vox, *but we think we need a more Afghan tone to the programme. We need you to dress in a more modest tradition.*"'

FAROOK. 'You're overreacting. Let me look.'

SAMIA. 'Overreacting? Easy for you to say. I haven't done anything wrong, but everyone hates me.'

FAROOK. 'Not everyone hates you.'

SAMIA. 'It should be my choice, it should always be my choice.'

FAROOK. 'There's nothing in here about being fired.'

SAMIA. 'Read between the lines this isn't a polite request.'

FAROOK. 'They wouldn't do that.'

SAMIA. 'It's their show.'

FAROOK. 'It's our show, we make it.'

SAMIA. 'So you would leave with me?'

FAROOK. 'I don't… It won't come to that.'

SAMIA. 'I think that says it all. They're winning, the old men. The fundamentalists, with their fundamentalist ways. Scaring everyone.'

FAROOK. 'But it's not just old men, is it?'

SAMIA. 'Backwards.'

FAROOK. 'Maybe you should just do it.'

SAMIA. 'What?'

*Beat.*

FAROOK. 'Someone threw a rock at my head on my way in.'

SAMIA. 'Are you alright?'

FAROOK. 'They missed. I couldn't see who it was. And with Jamie, and your brother. Just for a while, just until things have calmed down outside and we get back to normal.'

SAMIA. 'And when will that be? I won't go back, I can't go back, not to that. That's what they want.'

FAROOK. 'Afghanistan is moving forward, but it takes time.'

SAMIA. 'You were in Pakistan.'

FAROOK. 'What?'

SAMIA. 'You were in Pakistan, when it got so bad you got to escape. I was here the whole time.'

FAROOK. 'That's not fair, the refugee camp wasn't a hotel.'

SAMIA. 'My mother went crazy in the house, inside all day, every day. She didn't die waiting in the corridor of the one hospital in the whole city that was allowed to treat women. She died long before then.

I won't be my mother.'

FAROOK. 'It won't come to that, let's just do what they say, for a while. Things will get better again.'

SAMIA. 'You can promise that?'

FAROOK. I really believed they would. So I just say 'Of course'.

SAMIA. And I believe you?

FAROOK. You trust me. We're friends. Why wouldn't you?

I never actually told you, but you were my best friend. Was I yours?

SAMIA. I don't do soppy emotions.

FAROOK. I know.

SAMIA. And you know I can't answer that.

FAROOK. I really wish you could.

SAMIA *puts on a covering over her hair.*

*On-air:*

We just have enough time to play the retro track that has been suggested by you at home.

SAMIA. This one has a dance to it as well. We should do the dance.

FAROOK. No. I don't think… we don't have time.

SAMIA. We'll be quick, here's the music –

*'Macarena' by Los Del Rio comes on.*

– you know what it is –

FAROOK. – the 'Macarena' –

SAMIA. You know the dance…

FAROOK. Cool.

SAMIA. I love this dance. It's so good. Come on!

*They do a round of the Macarena, both with a smile on their faces.*

Enough now, here is the video and see you next time on *VOX*!

*Off-air:*

SAMIA *takes the covering off.*

FAROOK. And that was it.

SAMIA. 'Gyrating on screen with a man.'

FAROOK. I should have stopped you.

SAMIA. I do what I want.

FAROOK. But I should have. I should've stopped you. I should have stopped all of it. I shouldn't have been so oblivious, such a fool.

SAMIA. Then there would have been no *Vox*.

FAROOK. I think about all this, all these moments. Again and again. Did you know? Was this you saying: Forget the consequences?

SAMIA. It wasn't even the first time we'd done the Macarena, they're obviously not fans of the show. But you know it's bigger than this moment, it was all of it, the clothes, the hair, the music, us. This is just what they needed to latch on to, the excuse they had been looking for.

The clerics of the country had never been a fan of our show, they were the fringe and we were the norm. Right?

FAROOK. We were living in a bubble, the world outside had regressed and we were too slow to notice.

In the newspaper, Fazal Hadi Shinwari, a chief justice of the Afghan Supreme Court. Said that *Vox*:

SAMIA. 'Will corrupt our society, culture and most importantly, it will take our people away from Islam and destroy our country… This will make our people accept another culture, and make our country a laughing stock around the world.'

FAROOK. There it was in black and white. This wasn't a fringe voice, a backwards conservative condemning *Vox*. He was a mainstream opportunist. In the same article Asif had also made a statement.

SAMIA. 'Asif Noorzai Productions, makers of the show, insist they have nothing to do with the editorial content of the show.' Traitor.

FAROOK/ASIF. 'I warned you kids and I have a family to consider.'

SAMIA. As if we had no family at all.

FAROOK. TOLO TV was no better: '*Vox* doesn't reflect the values of the station so the future of the show is on review.'

SAMIA. Our show was now a matter of national importance. We were the centre of the storm. All alone.

FAROOK. Why did I think it was different for us? I want to shout: 'You idiot! What made you think you can help shift this country, when every side is against you? You're not special.' But I can't. I can't change a thing.

SAMIA. In the end it wouldn't have mattered.

FAROOK. You don't know that, it could have been different.

SAMIA. When it's written it's written.

Monday…

*On-air:*

FAROOK. We've been asking for tracks with a mad title, apparently we've played too much Britney this week. So no 'You Drive Me Crazy' instead this week's track is 'I Drive Myself Crazy' from NSYNC... Did you know that Joey the fat one from NSYNC is actually called Joey Fatone, spelt F-A-T-O-N-E. That's why Allah says be careful what you name your kids. Anyways here is the track.

*Off-air:*

She could be sick, maybe she lost her phone... No need to worry. There is a simple explanation. She'll be back tomorrow. I compose an SMS: 'The show was much better without you, THE STAR back where he belongs centre stage.' I hit send.

SAMIA. Tuesday...

FAROOK. I've called a dozen times,

SAMIA. 'You've got through to Sammy, I'm not here right now. I am most likely doing something super-fun and exciting, I know sucks to be me, leave a message.'

FAROOK. I leave more messages and send more SMSs. Asif tries too. Should I go to her house? Asif says no and for once I listen.

*On-air:*

Hey, my little Voxers, did you enjoy your commercial break? Now it's time to get back to the rocking tunes. And now I have a Bollywood blockbuster track that never sounds old!! It's the super-hit 'Muqabla Muqabla'!

*Song.*

I'm nine, and the fight has been between the Soviets and the Mujahideen. Walking home from school a landmine explodes. The force, like being shaken from the inside out... I still have a scar where the shrapnel lodged in my leg. But what they don't tell you about is the ringing in your ears.

For days all I hear is the metal clanging in my head. No silence, no peace. The doctor couldn't guarantee that my hearing would ever go back to normal. I listen to music or the noise from the TV to distract from the incessant ringing. It's this song on repeat for days.

My mother tells me about the producer of the track and India's most famous A. R. Rahman. He converted to Islam, after his sister was saved from dying by the prayers of an imam. My mother tells me to do the same. So I do, I pray every namaz.

The ringing did stop, and so had my prayers, no longer five times a day. But now I am praying, I am praying a lot, I'm praying for you.

SAMIA. Wednesday…

FAROOK. A voice message on my phone. Left from a number I don't recognise. The faint breath of someone on the other end of the line and then a scream… A woman, desperate, feral, guttural, like an animal taking its last breath, it hardly sounded human. Just for a few seconds, then gone.

*la ilaha illa muhammadur rasulullah*

Please don't be her.

*la ilaha illa muhammadur rasulullah*

Please don't be her.

Rumours spread about Samia, she is missing and what has happened. Management has decided that we should address this directly.

*On-air:*

We have had so many messages asking where VJ Sammy is… Don't panic, my Voxers, she is just unwell, and sick in her bed. Get well soon, Samia!!! We're all thinking of you here at *Vox*, all care for you and want you to be safe and well and are praying for you. Come back soon…

Sorry, what was next? That's right we're playing, 'What Would You Rather?' And today's conundrum: Would you rather lick a toilet seat every day for a week or not shower for a year.

*Off-air:*

SAMIA. Thursday...

FAROOK. Nothing. Her phone doesn't ring any more. Straight to voicemail, too full to leave messages. Her brothers, father, friends, no one has heard a thing. Six days... She was last seen on Saturday.

I tell the police about the message on my phone. They just sit on their asses. I pray but the hope is gone. And still the show must go on.

*On-air:*

It's that time of the week, time to announce our new number one, drumroll please... and it's 'Buttons' from The Pussycat Dolls. They are super-talented! And now they are also this week's new number one. We can only play the edited video. So I thought why don't we chat to a massive PCD fan first, so we have Mahmood on the line:

Hey Mahmood.

SAMIA. Should I?

FAROOK. You don't have to.

SAMIA. Who else is there?

FAROOK. No one.

SAMIA/MAHMOOD. Hello.

FAROOK. So you are the biggest Pussycat Doll fan in Kabul?

SAMIA/MAHMOOD. Yes.

FAROOK. Why do you think they're so great?

SAMIA/MAHMOOD. Good music.

FAROOK. Okay. And who is your favourite member?

SAMIA/MAHMOOD. All of them.

FAROOK. Really? My favourite has to be Nicole.

SAMIA/MAHMOOD. She is dark.

FAROOK. But dark people can be pretty too and she can really sing and dance. Do you want to introduce the song and our new number one?

*Silence.*

Mahmood… have we lost you? Are you still there?

SAMIA/MAHMOOD. Yes. Can I tell a joke?

FAROOK. Well, you've not exactly been a barrel of laughs.

SAMIA/MAHMOOD. What did the whore say when she crossed the road?

FAROOK. I don't think that is an appropriate joke.

SAMIA/MAHMOOD. Please don't kill me. She said please don't kill me.

*Inna lillahi wa inna ilayhi raji'un (Islamic prayer for the dead).*

You're next…

FAROOK *stands there. paralysed, as 'Buttons' by The Pussycat Dolls' begins to play around him. After a couple of bars he snaps back into action.*

FAROOK. The Pussycat Dolls with 'Buttons', everybody. And then next is the news on TOLO TV… See you next time… on *VOX*!

*Off-air:*

Asif rushes into the studio, he's saying something but I don't hear him. I hear the prayer for the dead in my head on loop.

'Why did you let him on the show? You, you know something, don't you, Asif, protecting yourself, by offering us to slaughter.'

He slaps me hard, I bite my tongue, I can taste blood in my mouth. I sob, in a voice I don't recognise as my own.

SAMIA. Friday…

FAROOK. They find her body one kilometre from her house, shot in the head and she had been interfered with.

SAMIA. What does that mean? Interfered with.

FAROOK. Don't make me say it.

SAMIA. No.

FAROOK. I'm sorry.

SAMIA. No, fuck you and fuck this story.

FAROOK. This isn't a story, these are the facts.

SAMIA. So why am I here?

FAROOK. Because I wanted them to know you, as much as I did. I tried to bring you back to life as much as I could, as much as I know. My friend. My beautiful friend.

SAMIA. So you could have me killed again. Change the story.

FAROOK. I can't, I wish I could. I really wish I could.

SAMIA. No. NO!

That scream you heard on the phone, that wasn't me! That wasn't mine!

There are two of them, big burly men, leading me deep into the forest. I'm calm, never afraid, never weak. I see my chance. I kick one so hard in the groin he falls to the floor, barely able to breathe. He's in agony, frothing at the mouth. I bite the other's hand. I bite so hard I draw blood and spit out his flesh. He was the one who screamed like a defenceless woman. Not me.

And I run. Run through the forest. Run so fast they can barely keep up. There are hundreds of different paths I could take, all leading in different directions, different endings, different lives lived. I look down one and I see myself old

with my grandchildren around me, I'm telling them about
how I was a presenter on TV. Another shows me on a plane,
I'm in the USA interviewing Britney about her latest release.
The other, I have just been elected as an MP fighting for
women's rights, I see myself as the author of an international
bestseller, an entrepreneur, a director of movies, a teacher, an
activist, President of Afghanistan.

But two more men appear and I'm surrounded. Four of them
and one of me. Cowards.

One of them pulls out a gun and points it at my face. Orders
me to my knees.

'Never.'

I don't plead and I don't beg. I stand up taller than I ever
have, I look him straight in the eyes.

'Pull the trigger, you motherfucker, I'm not scared of you.
DO IT!'

He is the one whimpering and I am resolute. He pulls the
trigger. In between my eyes. BANG!

I don't feel a thing.

What they do to my body after doesn't matter, because it's
not me. I'm already gone.

SAMIA *leaves the space*.

FAROOK. At fourteen thirty the decision is made to cancel *Vox*
indefinitely. And just like that everything is gone…

*On-air:*

Welcome to this special edition of *VOX*!!!

You thought they'd cancelled the show??

Well, how could they cancel the show, when the star is still
here.

I've spent the last forty days living in isolation in this studio
– can you imagine that? The only place that I can be offered

protection, they have guards. Here, let me take you on a tour of my lodgings...

This bucket, what's it even doing in the studio? BUT it's not a bucket, it's a luxury toilet – yes, this is where I piss and shit.

Where do you bathe, Farook? I have a tiny sink, for all my needs, drinking and bathing.

When I need to stretch my legs I walk around, ample grounds... around and around and around. Until I want to vomit... but don't worry, I have my bucket.

And I can eat as much pizza as I like, as they are the only ones who will deliver. And guess what? I fucking hate pizza now!!

This corner here is my bedroom.

I think it's time to read some texts from our viewers:

'You're next you pig.

We will find you and kill you and your whole family.

I'm gonna fuck you like we fucked that whore.'

I think that's enough of that don't you, my little Voxers.

Now it's time to call one of our lucky viewers, he's not any viewer, he's really important...

*Makes a call.*

Straight to answerphone, AGAIN... should I leave another message? Why not?

'Mr Hamidi, remember you gave me your cell number and said how proud you were of the show and if I ever needed anything just to call. Well, I need your help. Please, please call me back, you fucking motherfucking son of a bitch. BYEEEE.'

That, folks, was the head of the station, Mr Hamidi... long-time fan of the show.

Maybe I should call my mother next, but what if they trace the call and find her. SO I WON'T, I won't speak to anyone I love because what if they hunt them down and kill them?

They've done it before and they can do it again.

A game! A brand-new game… What's this one called? The Wheel of Fortune. But there is no wheel. Can't you see it, it's right here. Let me take my first spin. What's the prize you ask? Freedom.

*Spins.*

Oh where is it going to land?

Afghan police:

Can you help me, Afghan police?

NO – 'Because you deserve everything you get, you Hazara.'

The same police who say the murder of my friend is an honour killing, so they don't have to investigate it.

Take another spin.

US embassy:

Can you help me, USA?

NO – 'Because we've won the war, it's safe here, you're now free.'

Thank you for my freedom, I'm not sure it's the kind of liberty your people would accept. Bastards… use me and then what?

One more spin, my last one. I hope it's a good one.

British embassy:

Can you help me?

NO – 'If we let you in we will have to let everyone in.'

I forget you only like sending your people to take over countries, you never return the favour. Well, fuck you very much, UK.

BONUS QUESTION!!

Is Asif a traitor? Where are you? Come on, Asif, come answer this question. He's not here. He's safe with his family.

He's letting me stay here. So he can't be. Can he? Yet he
always hated us. Did you see this coming or did you betray
us? What if you betray me now, what if they get to you?
Threaten your family, and you offer me instead. And I'm just
sat here... waiting. I need to leave but where? What do I do?
Who can I trust? The truth is you can't trust anyone ever...

The only person you have is yourself.

Look at me, why so glum?? We need MUSIC. Yes. yes.
Some music.

I still have all my tunes. Lucky, lucky me.

Let's choose one at random.

*'...Baby One More Time' starts playing.*

NO NO not this song please, please not this song. NO. Make
it stop. Make it stop.

*There is a stark shift of time and place.*

Stop this. Please, stop this!

*The music abruptly cuts out.*

Someone make it... stop!

*Pause as* FAROOK *realises the music has stopped and
regains composure.*

The Britney track is no longer playing and I realise where
I am. Everyone's eyes are on me. I decide I should go. I walk
towards the door in silence, through a mass of people, none
of whom look like me, all staring. And it's nothing like the
videos. This party. Nobody's dancing and they don't even
listen to pop.

I walk out the door and the cold hits me in the face.
Denmark. This is where I live now.

What can I tell you about Denmark? It is cold... I have to
have the heating on all the time and still I'm wearing a
jumper. The population is five million, a country a little
bigger than the city of Kabul.

I never really thought about Denmark, it was always USA, USA.

But here I am, on my way 'home'. I swapped the container of a studio for a container of an apartment. They literally took old metal containers and turned them into flats for people like me: 'asylum seekers'. That's my new title, not as catchy as 'VJ'.

I got myself a job, there is not much call for Afghan TV presenters in Copenhagen, but cleaners, that's a growth sector. I'm left alone and I get paid in cash. Asif sent me some money too, we spoke on the phone, which was nice.

It is so different here, the people. Today was the first time I had spoken to anyone in four days. That's a new record for me.

And I'm made to go to college, but I make no friends. I prefer to remain quiet and just watch everyone else. That's where I was invited to this party. I forced myself to go, I even put gel in my hair. I have never felt so alone in a room full of people. I feel so old. Three years since we started *Vox*, feels like a lifetime.

Finally a girl speaks to me, 'What music do you like?' I want to say 'Who cares?', but I automatically respond: 'I like pop the best and my favourite is Britney'. She laughs at me.

She was the one who put Britney on as a joke.

*'...Baby One More Time' plays faintly in the background.*

And it all came flooding back.

SAMIA *re-emerges*.

Did you know 'hit me baby one more time', it has like a *sexual* meaning too.

SAMIA. How are you?

FAROOK. I don't sleep. I miss Afghanistan every day.

*Beat.*

I'm sorry.

SAMIA. You have nothing to be sorry for.

FAROOK. I'm alive and you are not.

SAMIA. When it's written, it's written.

*Beat.*

FAROOK. You were my best friend.

SAMIA. You were mine too.

'My loneliness is killing me (and I)
I must confess I still believe (still believe)
When I'm not with you I lose my mind
Give me a sign
Hit me, baby, one more time'

*The End.*

**A Nick Hern Book**

*Kabul Goes Pop: Music Television Afghanistan* first published in Great Britain in 2022 as a paperback original by Nick Hern Books Limited, The Glasshouse, 49a Goldhawk Road, London W12 8QP, in association with Brixton House, HighTide and Mercury Theatre Colchester

*Kabul Goes Pop: Music Television Afghanistan* copyright © 2022 Waleed Akhtar

Cover image: Azarra Amoy

Designed and typeset by Nick Hern Books, London
Printed in Great Britain by Mimeo Ltd, Huntingdon, Cambridgeshire PE29 6XX

A CIP catalogue record for this book is available from the British Library

ISBN 978 1 83904 093 1